"'Tis Sixty Year

Address of Charles Francis Adams
Founders' Day, January 16, 1913

Charles Francis Adams

Alpha Editions

This edition published in 2023

ISBN : 9789362098313

Design and Setting By
Alpha Editions
www.alphaedis.com
Email - info@alphaedis.com

"'TIS SIXTY YEARS SINCE"

In the single hour self-allotted for my part in this occasion there is much ground to cover,--the time is short, and I have far to go. Did I now, therefore, submit all I had proposed to say when I accepted your invitation, there would remain no space for preliminaries. Yet something of that character is in place. I will try to make it brief.[1]

As the legend or text of what I have in mind to submit, I have given the words "'Tis Sixty Years Since." As some here doubtless recall, this is the second or subordinate title of Walter Scott's first novel, "Waverley," which brought him fame. Given to the world in 1814,--hard on a century ago,--"Waverley" told of the last Stuart effort to recover the crown of Great Britain,--that of "The '45." It so chances that Scott's period of retrospect is also just now most appropriate in my case, inasmuch as I entered Harvard as a student in the year 1853--"sixty years since!" It may fairly be asserted that school life ends, and what may in contradistinction thereto be termed thinking and acting life begins, the day the young man passes the threshold of the institution of more advanced education. For him, life's responsibilities then begin. Prior to that confused, thenceforth things with him become consecutive,--a sequence. Insensibly he puts away childish things.

[1] Owing to its length, this "Address" was compressed in delivery, occupying one hour only. It is here printed in the form in which it was prepared,--the parts omitted in delivery being included.

In those days, as I presume now, the college youth harkened to inspired voices. Sir Walter Scott belonged to a previous generation. Having held the close attention of a delighted world as the most successful story-teller of his own or any preceding period, he had passed off the stage; but only a short twenty years before. Other voices no less inspired had followed; and, living, spoke to us. Perhaps my scheme to-day is best expressed by one of these.

When just beginning to attract the attention of the English-speaking world, Alfred Tennyson gave forth his poem of "Locksley Hall,"--very familiar to those of my younger days. Written years before, at the time of publication he was thirty-three. In 1886, a man of seventy-five, he composed a sequel to his earlier effort,--the utterance entitled "Locksley Hall Sixty Years After." He then, you will remember, reviewed his young man's dreams,--dreams of the period when he

" ... dip't into the future, far as human eye could see, Saw the Vision of the world, and all the wonder that would be,"

--threescore years later contrasting in sombre verse an old man's stern realities with the bright anticipations of youth. Such is my purpose to-day. "Wandering back to living boyhood," to the time when I first simultaneously passed the Harvard threshold and the threshold of responsible life, I propose to compare the ideals and actualities of the present with the ideals, anticipations and dreams of a past now somewhat remote.

To say that in life and in the order of life's events it is the unexpected which is apt to occur, is a commonplace. That it has been so in my own case, I shall presently show. Meanwhile, not least among the unexpected things is my presence here to-day. If, when I entered Harvard in 1853, it had been suggested that in 1913, I,--born of the New England Sanhedrim, a Brahmin Yankee by blood, tradition and environment-- had it been suggested that I, being such, would sixty years later stand by invitation here in Columbia before the faculty and students of the University of South Carolina, I should under circumstances then existing have pronounced the suggestion as beyond reasonable credence. Here, however, I am; and here, from this as my rostrum, I propose to-day to deliver a message,--such as it is.

And yet, though such a future outcome, if then foretold, would have seemed scarcely possible of occurrence, there, after all, were certain conditions which would have rendered the contingency even at that time not only possible, but in accordance with the everlasting fitness of things. For, curiously enough, personal relations of a certain character held with this institution would have given me, even in 1853, a sense of acquaintance with it such as individually I had with no other institution of similar character throughout the entire land. It in this wise came about. At that period, preceding as it did the deluge about to ensue, it was the hereditary custom of certain families more especially of South Carolina and of Louisiana,--but of South Carolina in particular--to send their youth to Harvard, there to receive a college education. It thus chanced that among my associates at Harvard were not a few who bore names long familiarly and honorably known to Carolinian records,-- Barnwell and Preston, Rhett and Alston, Parkman and Eliot; and among these were some I knew well, and even intimately. Gone now with the generation and even the civilization to which they belonged, I doubt if any of them survive. Indeed only recently I chanced on a grimly suggestive mention of one who had left on me the memory of a character and personality singularly pure, high-toned and manly,-- permeated with a sense of moral and personal obligation. I have always understood he died five years later at Sharpsburg, as you call it, or Antietam, as it was named by us, in face-to-face conflict with a Massachusetts regiment largely officered by Harvard men of his time and even class,--his own familiar friends. This is the record, the reference being to a marriage service held at St. Paul's church in Richmond, in the late autumn of 1862: "An indefinable feeling of gloom was thrown over a most auspicious event when the bride's youngest sister glided through a side door just before the processional. Tottering to a chancel pew, she threw herself upon the cushions, her slight frame racked with sobs. Scarcely a year before, the wedding march had been played for her, and a joyous throng saw her wedded to gallant Breck Parkman. Before another twelvemonth rolled around the groom was killed at the front."[2] Samuel Breck Parkman was in the Harvard class following that to which I belonged. Graduating in 1857, fifty-five years later I next saw his name in the connection just given. It recorded an incident of not infrequent occurrence in those dark and cruel days.

It was, however, in Breck Parkman and his like that I first became conscious of certain phases of the South Carolina character which subsequently I learned to bear in high respect.

So far as this University of South Carolina was concerned, it also so chanced that, by the merest accident, I, a very young man, was thrown into close personal relations with one of the most eminent of your professors,--Francis Lieber. Few here, I suppose, now personally remember Francis Lieber. To most it gives indeed a certain sense of remoteness to meet one who, as in my case, once held close and even intimate relations with a German emigrant, distinguished as a publicist, who as a youth had lain, wounded and helpless, a Prussian recruit, on the field above Namur. Occurring in June, 1815, two days after Waterloo, the affair at Namur will soon be a century gone. Of those engaged in it, the last obeyed the fell sergeant's summons a half score years ago. It seems remote; but at the time of which I speak Waterloo was appreciably nearer those in active life than are Shiloh and Gettysburg now. The Waterloo campaign was then but thirty-eight years removed, whereas those last are fifty now; and, while Lieber was at Waterloo, I was myself at Gettysburg.

[2] DeLeon, "Belles, Beaux and Brains of the Sixties," p. 158.

Subsequently, later in life, it was again my privilege to hold close relations with another Columbian,--an alumnus of this University as it then was--in whom I had opportunity to study some of the strongest and most respect-commanding traits of the Southern character. I refer to one here freshly remembered,--Alexander Cheves Haskell,--soldier, jurist, banker and scholar, one of a septet of brothers sent into the field by a South Carolina mother calm and tender of heart, but in silent suffering unsurpassed by any recorded in the annals whether of Judea or of Rome. It was the fourth of the seven Haskells I knew, one typical throughout, in my belief, of what was best in your Carolinian development. With him, as I have said, I was closely and even intimately associated through years, and in him I had occasion to note that almost austere type represented in its highest development in the person and attributes of Calhoun. Of strongly marked descent, Haskell was, as I have always supposed, of a family and race in which could be observed those virile Scotch-Irish and Presbyterian qualities which found their representative types in the two Jacksons,--Andrew, and him known in history as "Stonewall." To Alec Haskell I shall in this discourse again have occasion to refer.

Thus, though in 1853, and for long years subsequent thereto, it would not have entered my mind as among the probabilities that I should ever stand here, reviewing the past after the manner of Tennyson in his "Locksley Hall Sixty Years After," yet if there was any place in the South, or, I may say, in the entire country, where, as a matter of association, I might naturally have looked so to stand, it would have been where now I find myself.

But I must hasten on; for, as I have said, if I am to accomplish even a part of my purpose, I have no time wherein to linger.

Not long ago I chanced, in a country ramble, to be conversing with an eminent foreigner, known, and favorably known, to all Americans. In the course of leisurely exchange of ideas between us, he suddenly asked if I could suggest any explanation of the fact that not only were the publicists who had the greatest vogue in our college days now to a large extent discredited, but that almost every view and theory advanced by them, and which we had accepted as fixed and settled, was, where not actually challenged, silently ignored. Nor did the assertion admit of denial; for, looking back through the vista of threescore years, of the principles of what may be called "public polity" then advanced as indisputable, few to-day meet with general acceptance. To review the record from this point of view is curious.

When in 1853 I entered Harvard, so far as this country and its polity were concerned certain things were matters of contention, while others were accepted as axiomatic,--the basic truths of our system. Among the former--the subjects of active contention--were the question of Slavery, then grimly assuming shape, and that of Nationality intertwined therewith. Subordinate to this was the issue of Free Trade and

Protection, with the school of so-called American political economy arrayed against that of Adam Smith. Beyond these as political ideals were the tenets and theories of Jeffersonian Democracy. That the world had heretofore been governed too much was loudly acclaimed, and the largest possible individualism was preached, not only as a privilege but as a right. The area of government action was to be confined within the narrowest practical limits, and ample scope was to be allowed to each to develop in the way most natural to himself, provided only he did not infringe upon the rights of others. Materially, we were then reaching out to subdue a continent,--a doctrine of Manifest Destiny was in vogue. Beyond this, however, and most important now to be borne in mind, compared with the present the control of man over natural agencies and latent forces was scarcely begun. Not yet had the railroad crossed the Missouri; electricity, just bridled, was still unharnessed.

I have now passed in rapid review what may perhaps without exaggeration be referred to as an array of conditions and theories, ideals and policies. It remains to refer to the actual results which have come about during these sixty years as respects them, or because of them; and, finally, to reach if possible conclusions as to the causes which have affected what may not inaptly be termed a process of general evolution. Having thus, so to speak, diagnosed the situation, the changes the situation exacts are to be measured, and a forecast ventured. An ambitious programme, I am well enough aware that the not very considerable reputation I have established for myself hardly warrants me in attempting it. This, I premise.

Let us, in the first place, recur in somewhat greater detail to the various policies and ideals I have referred to as in vogue in the year 1853.

First and foremost, overshadowing all else, was the political issue raised by African slavery, then ominously assuming shape. The clouds foreboding the coming tempest were gathering thick and heavy; and, moreover, they were even then illumined by electric flashes, accompanied by a mutter of distant thunder. Though we of the North certainly did not appreciate its gravity, the situation was portentous in the extreme.

Involved in this problem of African slavery was the incidental issue of Free Trade and Protection,--apparently only economical and industrial in character, but in reality fundamentally crucial. And behind this lay the constitutional question, involving as it did not only the conflicting theories of a strict or liberal construction of the fundamental law, but nationality also,--the right of a Sovereign State to withdraw from the Union created in 1787, and developed through two generations.

These may be termed concrete political issues, as opposed to basic truths generally accepted and theories individually entertained. The theories were constitutional, social, economical. Constitutionally, they turned upon the obligations of citizenship. There was no such thing then as a citizen of the United States of and by itself. The citizen of the United States was such simply because of his citizenship of a Sovereign State,-- whether Massachusetts or Virginia or South Carolina; and, of course, an instrument based upon a divided sovereignty admitted of almost infinitely diverse interpretation. It is a scriptural aphorism that no man can serve two masters; for either he will hate the one and love the other, or else he will hold to the one and despise the other. And in the fulness of time it literally with us so came about. The accepted economical theories of the period were to a large extent corollaries of the fundamental proposition, and differing material and social conditions. Beyond all this, and coming still under the head of individual theories, was the doctrine enunciated by Thomas Jefferson in the Declaration of Independence,--the doctrine that all men were created equal,--meaning, of course, equal before the law. But the theorist and humanitarian of the North, accepting the fundamental principle laid down in the Declaration, gave to it a far wider application than had been intended by its authors,--a breadth of application it would not bear. Such science as he had being of scriptural origin, he interpreted the word "equal" as signifying equal in the possibilities of their attributes,--physical, moral, intellectual; and in so doing, he of course ignored the first principles of ethnology. It was, I now realize, a somewhat wild-eyed school of philosophy, that of which I myself was a youthful disciple.

But, on the other hand, beside these, between 1850 and 1860 a class of trained and more cautious thinkers, observers, scientists and theologians was coming to the front. Their investigations, though we did not then foresee it, were a generation later destined gently to subvert the accepted fundamentals of religious and economical thought, literary performance, and material existence. The work they had in hand to do was for the next fifteen years to be subordinate, so far as this country was concerned, to the solution of the terrible political problems which were first insistent on settlement; yet, as is now apparent, an initial movement was on foot which foreboded a revolution world-wide in its nature, and one in comparison with which the issues of slavery and American constitutionality became practically insignificant,--in a word, local and passing incidents.

Finally, it remains to consider specifically the political theories then in vogue in their relation to the individual. In this country, it was the period of the equality of man and individuality in the development of the type.

It was generally believed that the world had hitherto been governed too much,--that the day of caste, and even class, was over and gone; and finally, that America was a species of vast modern melting-pot of humanity, in which, within a comparatively short period of time, the characteristics of all branches of Indo-Aryan origin would resolve themselves. A new type would emerge,--the American. These theories were also in their consequences far-reaching. Practically, 1853 antedates all our present industrial organizations so loudly in evidence,--the multifarious trades-unions which now divide the population of the United States into what are known as the "masses" and the "classes." As recently as a century ago, it used to be said of the French army under the Empire, that every soldier carried the baton of the Field-Marshal in his knapsack. And this ideal of equality and individuality was fixed in the American mind.

Not that I for a moment mean to imply that in my belief the middle of the last century, or the twenty years anterior to the Civil War, was a species of golden age in our American annals. On the contrary, it was, as I remember it, a phase of development very open to criticism; and that in many respects. It was crude, self-conscious and self-assertive; provincial and formative, rather than formed. Socially and materially we were, compared with the present era of motors and parlor-cars, in the "one-hoss shay" and stove-heated railroad-coach stage. Nevertheless, what is now referred to as "predatory wealth" had not yet begun to accumulate in few hands; much greater equality of condition prevailed; nor was the "wage-earner" referred to as constituting a class distinct from the holders of property. Thus the individual was then encouraged,--whether in literature, in commerce, or in politics. In other words, there being a free field, one man was held to be in all respects the equal of the rest. Especially was what I have said true of the Northern, or so-called Free States, as contrasted with the States of the South, where the presence of African slavery distinctly affected individual theories, no matter where or to what extent entertained.

Such, briefly and comprehensively stated, having been the situation in 1853, it remains to consider the practical outcome thereof during the sixty years it has been my fortune to take part, either as an actor or as an observer, in the great process of evolution. It is curious to note the extent to which the unexpected has come about. In the first place, consider the all-absorbing mid-century political issue, that involving the race question, to which I first referred,--the issue which divided the South from the North, and which, eight years only after I had entered college, carried me from the walks of civil life into the calling of arms.

And here I enter on a field of discussion both difficult and dangerous; and, for reasons too obvious to require statement, what I am about to say will be listened to with no inconsiderable apprehension as to what next may be forthcoming. Nevertheless, this is a necessary part of my theme; and I propose to say what I have in mind to say, setting forth with all possible frankness the more mature conclusions reached with the passage of years. Let it be received in the spirit in which it is offered.

So far, then, as the institution of slavery is concerned, in its relations to ownership and property in those of the human species,--I have seen no reason whatever to revise or in any way to alter the theories and principles I entertained in 1853, and in the maintenance of which I subsequently bore arms between 1861 and 1865. Economically, socially, and from the point of view of abstract political justice, I hold that the institution of slavery, as it existed in this country prior to the year 1865, was in no respect either desirable or justifiable. That it had its good and even its elevating side, so far at least as the African is concerned, I am not here to deny. On the contrary, I see and recognize those features of the institution far more clearly now than I should have said would have been possible in 1853. That the institution in itself, under conditions then existing, tended to the elevation of the less advanced race, I frankly admit I did not then think. On the other hand, that it exercised a most pernicious influence upon those of the more advanced race, and especially upon that large majority of the more advanced race who were not themselves owners of slaves,--of that I have become with time ever more and more satisfied. The noticeable feature, however, so far as I individually am concerned, has been the entire change of view as respects certain of the fundamental propositions at the base of our whole American political and social edifice brought about by a more careful and intelligent ethnological study. I refer to the political equality of man, and to that race absorption to which I have alluded,--that belief that any foreign element introduced into the American social system and body politic would speedily be absorbed therein, and in a brief space thoroughly assimilated. In this all-important respect I do not hesitate to say we theorists and abstractionists of the North, throughout that long anti-slavery discussion which ended with the 1861 clash of arms, were thoroughly wrong. In utter disregard of fundamental, scientific facts, we theoretically believed that all men--no matter what might be the color of their skin, or the texture of their hair--were, if placed under exactly similar conditions, in essentials the same. In other words, we indulged in the curious and, as is now admitted, utterly erroneous theory that the African was, so to speak, an Anglo-Saxon, or, if you will, a Yankee "who had never had a chance,"--a fellow-man who was guilty, as we chose to express it, of a skin not colored like our own. In other words, though carved in ebony, he also was in the image of God.

Following out this theory, under the lead of men to whom scientific analysis and observation were anathema if opposed to accepted cardinal political theories as enunciated in the Declaration as read by them, the African was not only emancipated, but so far as the letter of the law, as expressed in an amended Constitution, would establish the fact, the quondam slave was in all respects placed on an equality, political, legal and moral, with those of the more advanced race.

I do not hesitate here,--as one who largely entertained the theoretical views I have expressed,--I do not hesitate here to say, as the result of sixty years of more careful study and scientific observation, the theories then entertained by us were not only fundamentally wrong, but they further involved a problem in the presence of which I confess to-day I stand appalled.

It is said,--whether truthfully or not,--that when some years ago John Morley, the English writer and thinker, was in this country, on returning to England he remarked that the African race question, as now existing in the United States, presented a problem as nearly, to his mind, insoluble as any human problem well could be. I do not care whether Lord Morley made this statement or did not make it. I am prepared, however, to say that, individually, so far as my present judgment goes, it is a correct presentation. To us in the North, the African is a comparatively negligible factor. So far as Massachusetts, for instance, or the city of Boston more especially, are concerned, as a problem it is solving itself. Proportionately, the African infusion is becoming less-- never large, it is incomparably less now than it was in the days of my own youth. Thus manifestly a negligible factor, it is also one tending to extinction. Indeed, it would be fairly open to question whether a single Afro-American of unmixed Ethiopian descent could now be found in Boston. That the problem presents itself with a wholly different aspect here in Carolina is manifest. The difference too is radical; it goes to the heart of the mystery.

As I have already said, the universal "melting-pot" theory in vogue in my youth was that but seven, or at the most fourteen, years were required to convert the alien immigrant--no matter from what region or of what descent--into an American citizen. The educational influences and social environment were assumed to be not only subtle, but all-pervasive and powerful. That this theory was to a large and even dangerous extent erroneous the observation of the last fifty years has proved, and our Massachusetts experience is sadly demonstrating to-day. It was Oliver

Wendell Holmes, who, years ago, when asked by an anxious mother at what age the education of a child ought to begin, remarked in reply that it should begin about one hundred and fifty years before the child is born. It has so proved with us; and the fact is to-day in evidence that this statement of Dr. Holmes should be accepted as an undeniable political aphorism. So far from seven or fourteen years making an American citizen, fully and thoroughly impregnated with American ideals to the exclusion of all others, our experience is that it requires at least three generations to eliminate what may be termed the "hyphen" in citizenship. Not in the first, nor in the second, and hardly in the third, generation, does the immigrant cease to be an Irish-American, or a French-American, or a German-American, or a Slavonic-American, or yet a Dago. Nevertheless, in process of tune, those of the Caucasian race do and will become Americans. Ultimately their descendants will be free from the traditions and ideals, so to speak, ground in through centuries passed under other conditions. Not so the Ethiopian. In his case, we find ourselves confronted with a situation never contemplated in that era of political dreams and scriptural science in which our institutions received shape. Stated tersely and in plain language, so far as the African is concerned--the cause and, so to speak, the motive of the great struggle of 1861 to 1865--we recognize the presence in the body politic of a vast alien mass which does not assimilate and which cannot be absorbed. In other words, the melting-pot theory came in sharp contact with an ethnological fact, and the unexpected occurred. The problem of African servitude was solved after a fashion; but in place of it a race issue of most uncompromising character evolved itself.

A survivor of the generation which read "Uncle Tom's Cabin" as it week by week appeared,--fresh to-day from Massachusetts with its Lawrence race issues of a different character, I feel a sense of satisfaction in discussing here in South Carolina this question and issue in a spirit the reverse of dogmatic, a spirit purely scientific, observant and sympathetic. And in this connection let me say I well remember repeatedly discussing it with your fellow-citizen and my friend, Colonel Alexander Haskell, to whom I have already made reference. Rarely have I been more impressed by a conclusion reached and fixed in the mind of one who to the study of a problem had obviously given much and kindly thought. As those who knew him do not need to be told, Alexander Cheves Haskell was a man of character, pure and just and thoughtful. He felt towards the African as only a Southerner who had himself never been the owner of slaves can feel. He regarded him as of a less advanced race than his own, but one who was entitled not only to just and kindly treatment but to sympathetic consideration. When, however, the question of the future of the Afro-American was raised, as matter for abstract discussion, it was suggestive as well as curious to observe the fixed, hard expression which immediately came over Haskell's face, as with stern lips, from which all suggestion of a smile had faded away, he pronounced the words:--"Sir, it is a dying race!" To express the thought more fully, Colonel Haskell maintained, as I doubt not many who now listen to me will maintain, that the nominal Afro-American increase, as shown in the figures of the national census, is deceptive,--that in point of fact, the Ethiop in America is incurring the doom which has ever befallen those of an inferior and less advanced race when brought in direct and immediate contact, necessarily and inevitably competitive, with the more advanced, the more masterful, and intellectually the more gifted. In other words, those of the less advanced race have a fatal aptitude for contracting the vices, both moral and physical, of the superior race, in the end leading to destruction; while the capacity for assimilating the elevating qualities and attributes which constitute a saving grace is denied them. Elimination, therefore, became in Haskell's belief a question of time only,--the law of the survival of the fittest would assert itself. The time required may be long,--numbered by centuries; but, however remotely, it nevertheless would come. God's mill grinds slowly, but it grinds uncommon small; and, I will add, its grinding is apt to be merciless.

The solution thus most pronouncedly laid down by Colonel Haskell may or may not prove in this case correct and final. It certainly is not for me, coming from the North, to undertake dogmatically to pass upon it. I recur to it here as a plausible suggestion only, in connection with my theme. As such, it unquestionably merits consideration. I am by no means prepared to go the length of an English authority in recently saying that "emancipation on two continents sacrificed the real welfare of the slave and his intrinsic worth as a person, to the impatient vanity of an immediate and theatrical triumph.">[3] This length I say, I cannot go; but so far as the present occasion is concerned, with such means of observation as are within my reach, I find the conclusion difficult to resist that the success of the abolitionists in effecting the emancipation of the Afro-American, as unexpected and sweeping as it was sudden, has led to phases of the race problem quite unanticipated at least. For instance, as respects segregation. Instead of assimilating, with a tendency to ultimate absorption, the movement in the opposite direction since 1865 is pronounced. It has, moreover, received the final stamp of scientific approval. This implies much; for in the old days of the "peculiar institution" there is no question the relations between the two races were far more intimate, kindly, and even absorptive than they now are.

[3]Bussell's (Dr. F.W.) "Christian Theology and Social Progress." Bampton Lectures, 1905.

That African slavery, as it existed in the United States anterior to the year 1862, presented a mild form of servitude, as servitude then existed and immemorially had almost everywhere existed, was, moreover, incontrovertibly proven in the course of the Civil War. Before 1862, it was confidently believed that any severe social agitation within, or disturbance from without, would inevitably lead to a Southern servile insurrection. In Europe this result was assumed as of course; and, immediately after it was issued, the Emancipation Proclamation of President Lincoln was denounced in unmeasured terms by the entire London press. Not a voice was raised in its defence. It was regarded as a measure unwarranted in civilized warfare, and a sure and intentional incitement to the horrors which had attended the servile insurrections of Haiti and San Domingo; and, more recently, the unspeakable Sepoy incidents of the Indian mutiny. What actually occurred is now historic. The confident anticipations of our English brethren were, not for the first time, negatived; nor is there any page in our American record more creditable to those concerned than the attitude held by the African during the fierce internecine struggle which prevailed between April, 1861, and April, 1865. In it there is scarcely a trace, if indeed there is any trace at all, of such a condition of affairs as had developed in the Antilles and in Hindustan. The attitude of the African towards his Confederate owner was submissive and kindly. Although the armed and masterful domestic protector was at the front and engaged in deadly, all-absorbing conflict, yet the women and children of the Southern plantation slept with unbarred doors,--free from apprehension, much more from molestation.

Moreover, as you here well know, during the old days of slavery there was hardly a child born, of either sex, who grew up in a Southern household of substantial wealth without holding immediate and most affectionate relations with those of the other race. Every typical Southern man had what he called his "daddy" and his "mammy," his "uncle" and his "aunty," by him familiarly addressed as such, and who were to him even closer than are blood relations to most. They had cared for him in his cradle; he followed them to their graves. Is it needful for me to ask to what extent such relations still exist? Of those born thirty years after emancipation, and therefore belonging distinctly to a later generation, how many thus have their kindly, if humble, kin of the African blood? I fancy I would be safe in saying not one in twenty.

Here, then, as the outcome of the first great issue I have suggested as occupying the thought and exciting the passions of that earlier period, is a problem wholly unanticipated,--a problem which, merely stating, I dismiss.

Passing rapidly on, I come to the next political issue which presented itself in my youth,--the constitutional issue,--that of State Sovereignty, as opposed to the ideal, Nationality. And, whether for better or worse, this issue, I very confidently submit, has been settled. We now, also, looking at it in more observant mood, in a spirit at once philosophical and historical, see that it involved a process of natural evolution which, under the conditions prevailing, could hardly result in any other settlement than that which came about. We now have come to a recognition of the fact that Anglo-Saxon nationality on this continent was a problem of crystallization, the working out of which occupied a little over two centuries. It was in New England the process first set in, when, in 1643, the scattered English-speaking settlements under the hegemony of the colony of Massachusetts Bay united in a confederation. It was the initial step. I have no time in which to enumerate successive steps, each representing a stage in advance of what went before. The War of Independence,--mistakenly denominated the Revolutionary War, but a struggle distinctly conservative in character, and in no way revolutionary,--the War of Independence gave great impetus to the process, resulting in what was known as Federation. Then came the Constitution of 1787 and the formation of the, so called, United States as a distinct nationality. The United States next passed through two definite processes of further crystallization,--one in 1812-1814, when the second war with Great Britain, and more especially our naval victories, kindled, especially in the North, the fire of patriotism and the conception of nationality; the other, half a century later, presented the stern issue in a concrete form, and at last the complete unification of a community-- whether for better or for worse is no matter--was hammered by iron and cemented in blood. It is there now; an established fact. Secession is a lost cause; and, whether for good or for ill, the United States exists, and will continue to exist, a unified World Power. Sovereignty now rests at Washington, and neither in Columbia for South Carolina nor in Boston for Massachusetts. The State exists only as an integral portion of the United States. That issue has been fought out. The result stands beyond controversy; brought about by a generation now passed on, but to which I belonged.

Meanwhile, the ancient adage, the rose is not without its thorn, receives new illustration; for even this great result has not been wrought without giving rise to considerations suggestive of thought. Speaking tersely and concentrating what is in my mind into the fewest possible words, I may say that in our national growth up to the year 1830 the play of the centrifugal forces predominated,--that is, the necessity for greater cohesion made itself continually felt. A period of quiescence then followed, lasting until, we will say, 1865. Since 1865, it is not unsafe to say, the centripetal, or gravitating, force has predominated to an extent ever more suggestive of increasing political uneasiness. It is now, as is notorious, more in evidence than ever before. The tendency to concentrate at Washington, the demand that the central government, assuming one function after another, shall become imperial, the cry for the national enactment of laws, whether relating to marital divorce or to industrial combinations,--all impinge on the fundamental principle of local self-government, which assumed its highest and most pronounced form in the claim of State Sovereignty. I am now merely stating problems. I am not discussing the political ills or social benefits which possibly may result from action. Nevertheless, all, I think, must admit that the tendency to gravitation and attraction is to-day as pronounced and as dangerous, especially in the industrial communities of the North, as was the tendency to separation and segregation pronounced and dangerous seventy years ago in the South.

To this I shall later return. I now merely point out what I apprehend to be a tendency to extremes--an excess in the swinging of our political pendulum.

We next come to that industrial factor which I have referred to as the issue between the Free Trade of Adam Smith and Protection, as inculcated by the so-called American school of political economists. The phases which this issue has assumed are, I submit, well calculated to excite the attention of the observant and thoughtful. I merely allude to them now; but, in so far as it is in my power to make it so, my allusion will be specific. I frankly acknowledge myself a Free-Trader. A Free-Trader in theory, were it in my power I would be a Free-Trader in national practice. There has been, so far as I know, but one example of absolute free trade on the largest scale in world history. That one example, moreover, has been a success as unqualified as undeniable. I refer to this American Union of ours. We have here a country consisting of fifty local communities, stretching from the Atlantic to the Pacific, from tropical Porto Rico to glacial Alaska, representing every conceivable phase of soil, climate and material conditions, with diverse industrial systems. With a Union established on the principle of absolutely unrestricted commercial intercourse, you here in South Carolina, and more especially in Columbia, are to-day making it, so to speak, uncomfortable for the cotton manufacturer in New England; and I am glad of it! A sharp competition is a healthy incentive to effort and ingenuity, and the brutal injunction, "Root hog or die!" is one from which I in no way ask to have New England exempt. When Massachusetts is no longer able to hold its own industrially in a free field, the time will, in my judgment, have come for Massachusetts to go down. With communities as with children, paternalism reads arrested development. One of the great products of Massachusetts has been what is generically known as "footwear." Yet I am told that under the operation of absolute Free Trade, St. Louis possesses the largest boot and shoe factory in its output in the entire world. That is, the law of industrial development, as natural conditions warrant and demand, has worked out its results; and those results are satisfactory. I am aware that the farmer of Massachusetts has become practically extinct; he cannot face the competition of the great West: but the Massachusetts consumer is greatly advantaged thereby. So far as agricultural products are concerned, Massachusetts is to-day reduced to what is known as dairy products and garden truck; and it is well! Summer vegetables manufactured under glass in winter prove profitable. So, turning his industrial efforts to that which he can do best, even the Massachusetts agriculturalist has prospered. On the other hand, wherever in this country protection has been most completely applied, I insist that if its results are analyzed in an unprejudiced spirit, it will be pronounced to have worked unmitigated evil,--an unhealthy, because artificially stimulated and too rapid, growth. Let Lawrence, in Massachusetts, serve as an example. Look at the industrial system there introduced in the name of Protection against the Pauper Labor of Europe! No growth is so dangerous as a too rapid growth; and I confidently submit that politically, socially, economically and industrially, America to-day, on the issues agitating us, presents an almost appalling example of the results of hot-house stimulation.

Nor is this all, nor the worst. There is another article, and far more damaging, in the indictment. Through Protection, and because of it, Paternalism has crept in; and, like a huge cancerous growth, is eating steadily into the vitals of the political system. Instead of supporting a government economically administered by money contributed by the People, a majority of the People to-day are looking to the government for support, either directly through pension payments or indirectly through some form of industrial paternalism. Incidentally, a profuse public expenditure is condoned where not actually encouraged. Jeffersonian simplicity is preached; extravagance is practised. As the New York showman long since shrewdly observed: "The American people love to be fooled!"

But I must pass on; I still have far to go. As respects legislation, I have said that sixty years ago, when my memories begin, the American ideal was the individual, and individuality. This, implied adherence to the Jeffersonian theory that heretofore the world had been governed too much. The great secret of true national prosperity, happiness and success was, we were taught, to allow to each individual the fullest possible play, provided only he did not infringe on the rights of others. How is it to-day? America is the most governed and legislated country in the world! With one national law-making machine perpetually at work grinding out edicts, we have some fifty provincial mills engaged in the same interesting and, to my mind, pernicious work. No one who has given the slightest consideration to the subject will dispute the proposition that, taking America as a whole, we now have twenty acts of legislation annually promulgated, and with which we are at our peril supposed to be familiar, where one would more than suffice. Then we wonder that respect for the law shows a sensible decrease! The better occasion for wonder is that it survives at all. We are both legislated and litigated out of all reason.

Passing to the other proposition of individuality, there has been, as all men know and no one will dispute, a most perceptible tendency of late years towards what is known as the array of one portion of the community--the preponderating, voting portion--against another--the more ostentatious property-holding portion. It is the natural result, I may say the necessary as well as logical outcome, of a period of too rapid growth,--production apportioned by no rule or system other or higher than greed and individual aptitude for acquisition. I will put the resulting case in the most brutal, and consequently the clearest, shape of which I am capable. Working on the combined theories of individualism controlled and regulated by competition, it has been one grand game of grab,--a process in which the whole tendency of our legislation, national or state, has during the last twenty years been, first, to create monopolies of capital and, later, to bring into existence a counter, but no less privileged, class, known as the "wage-earner."

Of the first class it is needless to speak, for, as a class, it is sufficiently pilloried by the press and from the hustings. Much in evidence, those prominent in it are known as the possessors of "predatory wealth"; "unjailed malefactors," they are subjects of continuous "grilling" in the congressional and legislative committee rooms. The effort to make them "disgorge" is as continual as it is noisy, and, as a rule, futile. It constitutes a curious and in some respects instructive exhibition of misdirected popular feeling and legislative incompetence. None the less, the existence of a monopolist class calls for no proof at the bar of public opinion. Not so the other and even more privileged class,--the so-called "wage-earner"; for, disguise it as the trades-unionist will, angrily deny it as he does, the fact remains that to-day under the operation of our jury system and of our laws, the Wage-earner and the member of the Trades-Union has become, as respects the rest of the community, himself a monopolist and, moreover, privileged as such. Practically, crimes urged and even perpetrated in behalf of so-called "labor" receive at the hands of juries, and also not infrequently of courts, an altogether excessive degree of merciful consideration. At the same time, both here and in Europe, Organized Labor is instant in its demand that immunity, denied to ordinary citizens, and those whom it terms "the classes," shall by special exemption be conferred upon the Labor Union and upon the Wage-earner. The tendency on both sides and at each extreme to inequality in the legislature and before the law is thus manifest.

Viewing conditions face to face and as they now are, no thoughtful observer can, in my judgment, avoid the conviction that, whether for good or ill, for better or for worse, this country as a community has, within the last thirty years--that is, we will say, since our centennial year, 1876--cast loose from its original moorings. It has drifted, and is drifting, into unknown seas. Nor is this true of English-speaking America alone. I have already quoted Lord Morley in another connection. Lord Morley, however, only the other day delivered, as Chancellor of Manchester University, a most interesting and highly suggestive address, in which, referring to conservative Great Britain, he thus pictured a phase of current belief: "Political power is described as lying in the hands of a vast and mobile electorate, with scanty regard for tradition or history. Democracy, they say, is going to write its own programme. The structure of executive organs and machinery is undergoing half-hidden but serious alterations. Men discover a change of attitude towards law as law; a decline in reverence for institutions as institutions."

While, however, the influences at work are thus general and the manifestations whether on the other side of the Atlantic or here bear a strong resemblance, yet difference of conditions and detail--constitutional peculiarities, so to speak--must not be disregarded. One form of treatment may not be prescribed for all. In our case, therefore, it remains to consider how best to adapt this country and ourselves to the unforeseeable,--the navigation of uncharted waters; and this adaptation cannot be considered hi any correct and helpful, because scientific, spirit, unless the cause of change is located. Surface manifestations are, in and of themselves, merely deceptive. A physician, diagnosing the chances of a patient, must first correctly ascertain, or at least ascertain with approximate correctness, the seat of the trouble under which the patient is suffering. So, we.

And here I must frankly confess to small respect for the politician,--the man whose voice is continually heard, whether from the Senate Chamber or the Hustings. There is in those of his class a continual and most noticeable tendency to what may best be described as the *post ergo propter* dispensation. With them, the eye is fixed on the immediate manifestation. Because one event preceded another, the first event is obviously and indisputably the cause of the later event. For instance, in the present case, the cause or seat of our existing and very manifest social, political and financial disturbances is attributed as of course to some peculiarity of legislation, either a subtreasury bill passed in the administration of General Jackson, or a tariff bill passed in the administration of Mr. Taft, or the demonetization of silver in the Hayes period,--that "Crime of the Century," the Crucifixion of Labor on the Cross of Gold! Once for all, let me say, I contemplate this school of politicians and so-called "thinkers" with sentiments the reverse of respectful. In plain language, I class them with those known in professional parlance as quacks and charlatans. Not always, not even in the majority of cases, does that which preceded bear to that which follows the relation of cause and effect. A marked example of this false attribution is afforded in more recent political history by the everlasting recurrence of the statement that American prosperity is the result of an American protective system. Yet in the Protectionist dispensation, this has become an article of faith. To my mind, it is undeserving of even respectful consideration.

If I were asked the cause of that change, little short of revolutionary, if indeed in any respect short of it, which has occurred in the material condition of the American people, and consequently in all its theories and ideals, within the last thirty years, I should attribute it to a wholly different cause. Mr. Lecky some years ago, in his book entitled "Liberty and Democracy," made the following statement, in no way original, but, as he put it, sufficiently striking: "The produce of the American mines [incident to the discoveries made by Columbus] created, in the most extreme form ever known in Europe, the change which beyond all others affects most deeply and universally the material well-being of men: it revolutionized the value of the precious metals, and, in consequence, the price of all articles, the effects of all contracts, the burden of all debts."

In other words, referring to the first half of the sixteenth century,--the sixty years, we will say, following the land-fall of Columbus,--the historian attributed the great change which then occurred and which stands forth so markedly in history, to the increased New-World production of the precious metals, combined with the impetus given to trade and industry as a consequence of that discovery, and of the mastery of man over additional globe areas. Now, dismissing from consideration the so-called American protective system, likewise our currency issues and, generally, the patchwork, so to speak, of crazy-quilt legislation to which so much is attributed during the last thirty years, I confidently submit that in the production of the results under discussion, they are quantities and factors hardly worthy of consideration. The cause of the change which has taken place lies far deeper and must be sought in influences of a wholly different nature, influences developed into an increased and still ever increasing activity, over which legislation has absolutely no control. I refer, of course, to man's mastery over the latent forces of Nature. Of these Steam and Electricity are the great examples, which, because always apparent, at once strike the imagination. These, as tools, it is to be remembered, date practically from within one hundred years back. It may, indeed, safely be asserted that up to 1815, the end of the Wars of Napoleon and the time of your Professor Lieber, steam even had not as yet practically affected the operations of man, while electricity, when not a terror, was as yet but a toy. Commerce was still exclusively carried on by the sailing ship and canal-boat. The years from the fall of Napoleon to our own War of Secession--from Waterloo to Gettysburg--were practically those of early and partial development. Not until well after Appomattox, that is, since the year 1870,--a period covering but little more than the life of a generation,--did what is known to you here as the Applied Sciences cover a range difficult to specialize. As factors in development, it is safe to say that those three tremendous agencies--Steam, Electricity, Chemistry--have, so to speak, worked all their noticeable results within the lifetime of the generation born since we celebrated the Centennial of Independence. The manifestations now resulting and apparent to all are the natural outcome of the use of these modern appliances, become in our case everyday working tools in the hands of the most resourceful, adaptive, ingenious and energetic of communities, developing a virgin continent of undreamed-of wealth. Naturally, under such conditions, the advance has been not only general and continuous, but one of ever increasing celerity. So Protection and the Currency become flies on the fast revolving wheel!

But what has otherwise resulted?--An unrest, social, economical, political. Not contentment, but a lamentation and an ancient tale of wrong! We hear it in the continual cry over what is known as the increased cost of living, and feel its pressure in the higher standard of living. What was considered wealth by our ancestors is to-day hardly competence. What sufficed for luxury in our childhood barely now supplies what are known as the comforts of life. Take, for instance, the motor,--the automobile. I speak within bounds, I think, when I say there are many fold more motors to-day racing over the streets, the highways and the byways of America than there were one-horse wagons thirty-five years ago. Six hundred, I am told, are to be found within the immediate neighborhood of Columbia; and, since I have been here I have seen in your streets just one man on horse-back! These figures and that statement tell the tale. A few years only back, every Carolinian rode to town, and the motor was unknown. A single illustrative example, this could be duplicated in innumerable ways everywhere and in all walks of life.

The result is obvious, and was inevitable. Entered on a new phase of existence, the world is not as it was in the days of Columbus, when a single new continent was discovered containing in it what we would now regard as a limited accumulation of the precious metals. It is, on the contrary, as if, in the language of Dr. Johnson, "the potentiality of wealth" had been revealed "beyond the dreams of avarice"; together with not one or two, but a dozen continents, the existence and secrets of which are suddenly laid bare. The Applied Sciences have been the magicians,--not Protection or the Currency.

And still scientists are continually dinning in our ears the question whether this state of affairs is going to continue,--whether the era of disturbance has reached its limit! I hold such a question to be little short of childish. That era has not reached its limits, nor has it even approximated those limits. On the contrary, we have just entered on the uncharted sea. We know what the last thirty years have brought about as the result of the agencies at work; but as yet we can only dimly dream of what the next sixty years are destined to see brought about. Imagination staggers at the suggestion.

What, then, has been of this the inevitable consequence,--the consequence which even the blindest should have foreseen? It has resulted in all those far-reaching changes suggested in the earlier part of what I have said to-day, as respects our ideals, our political theories, our social conditions. In other words, the old era is ended; what is implied when we say a new era is entered upon?

To attempt a partial answer to the query implies no claim to a prophetic faculty. Whether we like to face the fact or not, far-reaching changes in our economical theories and social conditions are imminent, involving corresponding readjustments in our constitutional arrangements and political machinery. Tennyson foreshadowed it all in his "Locksley Hall" seventy years ago:--"The individual withers, and the world is more and more." The day of individualism as it existed in the American ideal of sixty years since is over; that of collectivism and possibly socialism has opened. The day of social equality is relegated to what may be considered a somewhat patriarchal past,--that patriarchal past having come to a close during the memory of those still in active life.

And yet, though all this can now be studied in the political discussion endlessly dragging on, strangely and sadly enough that discussion carries in it hardly a note of encouragement. It is, in a word, unspeakably shallow. And here, having sufficiently for my present purpose though in hurried manner, diagnosed the situation,--located the seat of disturbance,--we come to the question of treatment. Involving, as it necessarily does, problems of the fundamental law, and a rearrangement and different allocation of the functions of government, this challenges the closest thought of the publicist. That the problem is here crying aloud for solution is apparent. The publications which cumber the counters of our book-stores, those for which the greatest popular call to-day exists--treatises relating to trade interests, to collectivism, to socialism, even to anarchism--tell the tale in part; in part it is elsewhere and otherwise told. Only recently, in once Puritan Massachusetts, processions paraded the streets carrying banners marked with this device, more suggestive than strange:--"No master and no God!"

What are the remedies popularly proposed? In that important branch of polity known as Political Ethics, or, as he termed them, Hermeneutics, which your Professor Lieber sixty years ago endeavored to treat of, what advance has since his time been effected?--Nay! what advance has been effected since the time, over two thousand years, of his great predecessor, Aristotle? I confidently submit that what progress is now being made in this most erudite of sciences is in the nature of that of the crab--backwards! In the discussions of Aristotle, the problem in view was, how to bring about government by the wisest,--that is, the most observant and expert. In other words, government, the object of politics, was by Aristotle treated in a scientific spirit. And this is as it should be. Take, for example, any problem,--I do not care whether it is legal or medical or one of engineering: How successfully dispose of it? Uniformly, in one way. Those problems are successfully solved, if at all, only when their solution is placed in the hands of the most proficient. Judged by the discussions of to-day, what advance has in politics been effected? Do the *Outlook* and the *Commoner* imply progress since the Stagirite? Not to any noticeable extent. We are, on the contrary, fumbling and wallowing about where the Greek pondered and philosophized.

Democracy, as it is called, is to-day the great panacea,--the political nostrum; as such it is confidently advocated by statesmen and professors and even by the presidents of our institutions of the advanced education.

"Trust the People" is the shibboleth! "Let the People rule!" "The cure for too much Liberty is more Liberty!" To Democracy plain and simple--Composite Wisdom--I frankly confess I feel no call,--no call greater than, for instance, towards Autocracy or Aristocracy or Plutocracy. Taken simply, and applied as hitherto applied, all and each lead to but one result,--failure! And that result, let me here predict, will, in the future, be the same in the case of pure Democracy that, in the past, it was in the case of the pure Autocracy of the Caesars, or the case of the pure Aristocracy of Rome or of the so-called Republics of the Middle Ages. A political edifice on shifting sands.

Yet, to-day what do we see and hear in America? Tell it not in Gath; publish it not in the streets of Askalon I Two thousand years after the time of Aristotle, we see a prevailing school working directly back to the condition of affairs which existed in the Athenian agora under the disapproving eyes of the father of political philosophy. Panaceas, universal cure-alls, and quack remedies--the Initiative, the Referendum, and the Recall are paraded as if these--nostrums of the mountebanks of the county fair--would surely remedy the perplexing ills of new and hitherto unheard-of social, economical, and political conditions. Democracy! What is Democracy? Democracy, as it is generally understood, I submit, is nothing but the reaching of political conclusions through the frequent counting of noses; or, as Macaulay two generations ago better phrased it, "the majority of citizens told by the head";--the only question at just this juncture being whether, in order to the arriving at more acceptable results, both sexes shall be "told," instead of one sex only. Moreover, I with equal confidence make bold to suggest that while conceded, and while men have even persuaded themselves that they have faith in it, and really do believe in this "telling" of noses as the best and fairest attainable means of reaching correct results, yet in so doing and so professing they simply, as men are prone to do, deceive themselves. In other words, victims of their own cant, they preach a panacea in which they really do not believe. Nor of this is proof far to seek. *Vox populi, vox Dei!* If you extend the application of this principle by a single step, its loudest advocates draw back in alarm from the inevitable. They seek refuge in the assertion--"Oh! That is different!" For instance, take a concrete case; so best can we illustrate.

One of the greatest scientific triumphs reached in modern times--perhaps I might fairly say the greatest--is the discovery of the cause of yellow fever, and its consequent control. As a result of the studies, the patient experimentation and self-sacrifice of the wisest,--that is, the most observant and expert,--the amazing conclusion was reached that not only the yellow fever but the innumerable ills of the flesh known under the caption of "malarial," were due to causes hitherto unsuspected, though obvious when revealed,--to the existence in the atmosphere of a venomous insect, in comparison with the work of which the ravages on mankind of the entire carnivorous and reptile creation were of comparatively small account. The mosquito flew disclosed, the atmospheric viper,--a viper most venomous and deadly. How was the disclosure brought about? What was the remedy applied? Was the discovery effected through universal suffrage? Was the remedy sought for and decided upon by the Initiative, or through a Referendum at an election held on the Tuesday succeeding the first Monday of a certain month and year? Had recourse in this case been had to the panacea now in greatest political vogue, we all know perfectly well what would have followed. History tells us. The quarantine, as it is called, would have been decreed, and a day of fasting, humiliation and prayer appointed. The mosquito, quite ignored, would then have gone on in his deadly work. We all equally well know that the man, even the politician or the statesman, who had suggested a solution of that problem by a count of noses would have been effaced with ridicule. Even the most simple minded would have rejected that method of reaching a result. Yet the ilia of the body politic, too, are complicated. Indeed, far more intricate in their processes and more deceitful in their aspects, they more deeply affect the general well-being and happiness than any ill or epidemic which torments the physical being, even the mosquito malaria. Yet the ills of the body politic, the complications which surround us on every side,--for these the unfailing panacea is said to lie in universal suffrage, that remedy which is immediately and of course laughed out of court if suggested in case of the simpler ills of the flesh.

This, I submit, is demonstration. The true remedy is not to be sought in that direction in the one case any more than the other.

There is a considerable element of truth, though possibly a not inconsiderable one of exaggeration, in this statement from a paper I recently chanced upon in the issue of the sober and classical *Edinburgh Review* for October last,--a paper entitled "Democracy and Liberalism":--"History testifies unmistakably and unanimously to the passion of democracies for incompetence. There is nothing democracy dislikes and suspects so heartily as technical efficiency, particularly when it is independent of the popular vote." But to-day, what is politically proposed by our senatorial charlatans and the mountebanks of the market-place? The Referendum, the constant and easy Recall, the everlasting Initiative are dinned into our ears as the cure-alls of every ill of the body politic. On the contrary, I submit that, while in the absence of any better method as yet devised and accepted, the process of reaching results by a count of the "majority told by the head" of the citizens then present and voting has certain political advantages, yet, for all this, as a final, scientific, political process, it is unworthy of consideration. A passing expedient, it in no degree reflects credit on twentieth-century intelligence.

And now I come to the crux of my discussion. Thus rejecting results reached by the ballot as now in practical use, a query is already in the minds of those who listen. At once suggesting itself and flung in my face, it is asked as a political poser, and not without a sneer,--What else or better have I to propose? Would I advise a return to old and discarded methods,--Heredity, Caste, Autocracy, Plutocracy? I respectfully submit this is a question no one has a right to put, and one I am not called upon to answer. Again, let me take a concrete case. Once more I appeal to the yellow fever precedent. The first step towards a solution of a medical, as of a political, problem is a correct diagnosis. Then necessarily follows a long period devoted to observation, to investigation and experiment. If, in the case of the yellow fever, a score of years only ago an observer had pointed out the nature of the disease and the manifest inadequacy of current theories and prevailing methods of prevention and treatment, do you think others would have had a right to turn upon him and demand that he instantly prescribe a remedy which should be not only complete, but at once recognized as such and so accepted? In the present case, as I have already observed, from the days of Aristotle down through two and twenty centuries, men had been experimenting in all, to them, conceivable ways, on the government of the body politic, exactly as they experimented on the disorders of the physical body. But only yesterday was the source of the yellow fever, for instance, diagnosed and located, and the proper means of prevention applied. The cancer and tuberculosis are to-day unsolved problems. By analogy, they are inviting subjects for an Initiative and a Referendum! Yet would any person who to-day, standing where I stand, expressed a disbelief, at once total and contemptuous, of such a procedure as respects them, be met by a demand for some other panacea of immediate and guaranteed efficiency? And so with the body politic. I here to-day am merely attempting a diagnosis, pointing out the disorders, and exposing as best I can the utter crudeness and insufficiency of the market-place remedies proposed. Have you a right, then, to turn on me, and call for some other prescription, warranted to cure, in place of the nostrums so loudly advertised by the sciolists and the dabblers of the day, and by me so contemptuously set aside? I confess I am unable to respond, or even to attempt a response to any such demand. I am not altogether a quack, nor is this a county fair.

"Paracelsus," so denominated, was one of Robert Browning's earlier poems. In it he causes the fifteenth-century alchemist and forerunner of all modern pharmaceutical chemistry, to declare that as the result of long travel and much research

"I possess
Two sorts of knowledge: one,--vast, shadowy,
Hints of the unbounded aim....
The other consists of many secrets, caught
While bent on nobler prize,--perhaps a few
Prime principles which may conduct to much:
These last I offer."

So, *longo intervallo*, I have a few suggestions,--the result of an observation extending, as I said at the beginning, over the lives of two generations and a connection with many great events in which I have borne a part,--a part not prominent indeed, and more generally, I acknowledge, mistaken than correct. My errors, however, have at least made me cautious and doubtful of my own conclusions. I submit them for what they are worth. Not much, I fear.

What, then, would I do, were it in my power to prescribe alterations and curatives for the ills of our American body politic, of which I have spoken; or, more correctly, the far-reaching disturbances manifestly due to the agencies at work, to which I have made reference? Let us come at once to the point, taking the existing Constitution of the United States as a concrete example, and recognizing the necessity for its revision and readjustment to meet radically changed conditions,--conditions social, material, geographical, changed and still changing.

It was Mr. Gladstone who, years ago, made the often-quoted assertion that the Constitution of the United States was "the most wonderful work ever struck off at a given time by the brain and purpose of man." I do not think he was far wrong; though we, of course, realize that the Federal Constitution was a growth and in no degree an inspiration. That Constitution has through a century and a quarter stood the test of time and stress of war, during a period of almost unlimited growth of the community for which it was devised. It has outlasted many nationalities and most of the dynasties in existence at the time of its adoption; and that, too, under conditions sufficiently trying. I, therefore, regard it with profound respect; and, so regarding it, I would treat it with a cautious and tender hand. Not lightly pronouncing it antiquated, what changes would I make in it if to-morrow it were given me to prescribe alterations adapting it to the altered conditions which confront us? I do not hesitate to say, and I am glad to say, the changes I would suggest would be limited; yet, I fancy, far-reaching.

And, in the first place, let us have a clear conception of the end in view. That end is, I submit, exactly the same to-day which Aristotle had in view more than twenty centuries ago. It is, not to solve all political problems, but to put political problems as they arise in the hands of those whom he termed the "best,"--but whom we know as the most intelligent, observant and expert,--to be, through their agency, in the way of ultimate solution. If, adopting every ill-considered and half-fledged measure of so-called reform which might be the fancy of the day, we incorporated them in our fundamental law, but one thing could result therefrom,--ultimate confusion. The Constitution is neither a legislative crazy-quilt nor a receptacle of fads. To make it such is in every respect the reverse of scientific. The work immediately in hand, therefore, is to devise such changes in the fundamental law as will tend most effectually to bring about the solution of issues as they may arise, by the most expert, observant and reliable. This accomplished, if its accomplishment were only practicable, all possible would have been done; and the necessary and inevitable readjustment of things would, in politics as in medicine and in science, be left to solve itself as occasion arose. Provision cannot be made against every contingency.

This premised, the Constitution of the United States is an instrument through which powers are delegated by several local communities to a central government. The instrument, it was originally held, should be strictly construed and the powers delegated limited; and in this respect, with certain alterations made obviously necessary to meet changed conditions, I would return to the fundamental idea of the framers.

In saying this I feel confidence also that here in South Carolina at least I shall meet with an earnest response. The time is not yet remote when local self-government worked salvation for South Carolina, as for her sister States of the Confederacy. You here will never forget what immediately followed the close of our Civil War. As an historic fact, the Constitution was then suspended. It was suspended by act of an irresponsible Congress, exercising revolutionary but unlimited powers over a large section of the common country. You then had an illustration, not soon to be forgotten, of concentration of legislative power. An episode at once painful and discreditable, it is not necessary here to refer to it in detail. Appeal, however, was made to the principle of local self-government,--it was, so to speak, a recurrence to the theory of State Sovereignty. The appeal struck a responsive, because traditional, chord; and it was through a recurrence to State Sovereignty as the agency of local self-government that loyalty and contentment were restored, and, I may add, that I am here to-day. Ceasing to be a Military Department, South Carolina once more became a State. Not improbably the demand will in a not remote future be heard that State lines and local autonomy be practically obliterated. In that event, I feel a confident assurance that, recurring in memory to the evil days which followed 1865, the spirit of enlightened conservatism will assert itself here and in the sister States of what was once the Confederacy; and again it will prevail. In the future, as in the past, you in South Carolina at least will cling to what in 1876 proved the ark of your social and political salvation.

Taking another step in the discussion of changes, the Constitution is founded on that well-known distribution and allocation of powers first theoretically suggested by Montesquieu. There is a division, accompanied by a mutual limitation of authority, through the Judiciary, the Executive, and the Legislative. As respects this allocation, how would I modify that instrument? I freely say that the tendency of my thought, based on observation, is to conservatism. I have never yet in a single instance found that when the people of this or any other country accustomed to parliamentary government desired a thing, they failed to obtain it within a reasonable limit of time. Hasty changes are wisely deprecated; but I think I speak within limitation when I say that neither in the history of Great Britain,--the mother of Parliaments--nor in the history of the United States, has any modification which the people, on sober second thought, have considered to be for the best, long been deferred. Action, revolutionary in character, has not, as a rule, been needful, or, when taken, proved salutary. This is a record and result that no careful student of our history will, I take it, deny.

Such being the case, so far as our Judiciary is concerned, I do not hesitate to say I would adhere to older, and, as I think, better principles, or revert to them where they have been experimentally abandoned. It took the Anglo-Saxon race two centuries of incessant conflict to wrest from a despotic executive, practically an autocracy, judicial independence. That was effected through what is known as a tenure during good behavior, as opposed to a tenure at the will of the monarch. This, then, for two centuries, was accepted as a fundamental principle of constitutional government. Of late, a new theory has been propounded, and by those chafing at all restraint--constitutionally lawless in disposition--it is said the Recall should also be applied to the Judiciary. Having, therefore, wrested the independence of the Judiciary from the hand of the Autocrat, we now propose to place it, in all trustfulness, in the hands of the Democrat. To me the proposition does not commend itself. It is founded on no correct principle, for the irresponsible democratic majority is even more liable to ill-considered and vacillating action than is the responsible autocrat. In that matter I would not trust myself; why, then, should I trust the composite Democrat? In the case of the Judiciary, therefore, I would so far as the fundamental law is concerned abide by the older and better considered principles of the framers.

Next, the Executive. Again, we hear the demand of Democracy,--the Recall! Once more I revert to the record. This Republic has now been in working operation, and, taken altogether, most successful operation, for a century and a quarter. During that century and a quarter we have had, we will say, some five and twenty different chief magistrates. There is an ancient and somewhat vulgar adage to the effect that the proof of a certain dietary article is in its eating. Apply that homely adage to the matter under consideration. What is the lesson taught? It is simply this,--during a whole century and a quarter of existence there has not been one single chief executive of the United States to whom the arbitrary Recall could have been applied with what would now be agreed upon as a fortunate result. In the Andrew Johnson impeachment case was it not better that things were as they were? On the other hand, every one of the seven independent, self-respecting Senators who then by a display of high moral courage saved the country from serious prejudice would have been recalled out-of-hand had the Recall now demanded been in existence. Its working would have received prompt exemplification; as it was, the recall was effected in time, and after due deliberation. The delay occasioned no public detriment. In this life, experience is undeniably worth something; and the experience here referred to is fairly entitled to consideration. No political system possible to devise is wholly above criticism,--not open to exceptional contingencies or to dangers possible to conjure up. Such have from time to time arisen in the past; in the future such will inevitably arise. This consideration must, however, be balanced against a general average of successful working; and I confidently submit that, weighing thus the proved advantage of the system we have against the possibilities of danger which hereafter may occur, but which never yet have occurred, the scale on which are the considerations in favor of change kicks the beam.

In view, however, of the growth of the country, the vastly increased complexity of interests involved, the intricacy and the cost of the election processes to which recourse is necessarily had, I would substitute for the present brief tenure of the presidential office--a tenure well enough perhaps in the comparatively simple days which preceded our Civil War--a tenure sufficiently long to enable the occupant of the presidential chair to have a policy and to accomplish at least something towards its adoption. As the case stands to-day, a President for the first time elected has during his term of four years, one year, and one year only, in which really to apply himself to the accomplishment of results. The first year of his term is necessarily devoted to the work of acquiring a familiarity with the machinery of the government, and the shaping of a policy. The second year may be devoted to a more or less strenuous effort at the adoption of the policy thus formulated. As experience shows, the action of the third and fourth years is gravely affected--if not altogether perverted from the work in hand -by what are known as the political exigencies incident to a succession. Manifestly, this calls for correction. The remedy, however, to my mind, is obvious and suggests itself. As the presidency is the one office under our Constitution national in character, and in no way locally representative, I would extend the term to seven years, and render the occupant of the office thereafter ineligible for reëlection. Seven years is, I am aware, under our political system, an unusual term; and here my ears will, I know, be assailed by the great "mandate" cackle. The count of noses being complete, the mind of the composite Democrat is held to be made up. It only remains to formulate the consequent decree; and, with least possible delay, put it in way of practical enforcement. Again, I, as a publicist, demur. It is the old issue, that between instant action and action on second thought, presented once more. Briefly, the experience of sixty years strongly inclines me to a preference of matured and considerate action over that immediate action which notoriously is in nine cases out of ten as ill-advised as it is precipitate. Only in the field of politics is the expediency of the latter assumed as of course; yet, as in science and literature and art so in politics, final, because satisfactory, results are at best but slowly thrashed out. As respects wisdom, the modern statute book does not loom, monumental. Its contemplation would indeed perhaps even lead to a surmise that reasonable delay in formulating his "mandate" might, in the case of the composite Democrat as in that of the individual Autocrat, prove a not altogether unmixed, and so in the end an intolerable, evil.

Thus while a change of the Executive and Legislative branches of the government might not be always simultaneously effected, by selecting seven years as the presidential term the election would be brought about, as frequently as might be, by itself, uncomplicated by local issues connected with the fortunes or political fate of individual candidates for office, whether State, Congressional, or Senatorial; and during the seven years of tenure, four, at least, it might reasonably be anticipated, would be devoted to the promotion of a definite policy, in place of one year in a term of four, as now. If also ineligible for reelection, there is at least a fair presumption that the occupant of the position might from start to finish apply himself to its duties and obligations, without being distracted therefrom by ulterior personal ends as constantly as humanly held in view.

Having thus disposed of the Judiciary and the Executive, we come to the Legislative. And here I submit is the weak point in our American system,--manifestly the weak point, and to those who, like myself, have had occasion to know, undeniably so. I am here as a publicist; not as a writer of memoirs: so, on this head, I do not now propose to dilate or bear witness. I will only briefly say that having at one period, and for more than the lifetime of a generation, been in charge of large corporate and financial interests, I have had much occasion to deal with legislative bodies, National, State and Municipal. That page of my experiences is the one I care least to recall, and would most gladly forget. I am not going to specify, or give names of either localities or persons; but, knowing what I know, it is useless to approach me on this topic with the usual good-natured and optimistic, if somewhat unctuous and conventional, commonplaces on general uprightness and the tendency to improved conditions and a higher standard. I know better! I have seen legislators bought like bullocks--they selling themselves. I have watched them cover their tracks with a cunning more than vulpine. I have myself been black-mailed and sandbagged, while whole legislative bodies watched the process, fully cognizant at every step of what was going on. This, I am glad to say, was years ago. The legislative conditions were then bad, scandalously bad; nor have I any reason to believe in a regeneration since. The stream will never rise higher than its source; but it generally indicates the level thereof. In this case, I can only hope that in my experience it failed so to do. Running at a low level, the waters of that stream were deplorably dirty.

That the legislative branch of our government has fallen so markedly in public estimation is not, I think, open to denial. To my mind, under the conditions I have referred to, such could not fail to be the case. It has, consequently, lost public confidence. Hence this popular demand for immediate legislation by the People,--this twentieth-century appeal to the Agora and Forum methods which antedate the era of Christ. It is true the world outgrew them two thousand years ago, and they were discarded; but, living in a progressive and not a reactionary period, all that, we are assured, is changed! The heart is no longer on the right-hand side of the body. To secure desired results it is only necessary to start quite fresh, as a mere preliminary discarding all lessons of experience.

Such reasoning does not commend itself to my judgment. On the contrary, the failure of the American legislative to command an increasing public confidence, while both natural and obvious, is, if my observation guides me to conclusions in any degree correct, traceable to two reasons. So far as government is concerned, the law-making branch is assumed to be made up of the wisest and the most expert. Meanwhile, it is as a matter of fact chosen by the process I have not over-respectfully referred to as the counting of noses; and, moreover, by an unwritten law more binding than any in the Statute Book, that counting of noses is with us localized. In other words, when it comes to the choice of our law-makers, reducing provincialism to a system we make the local numerical majority supreme, and any one is considered competent to legislate. He can do that, even if by common knowledge he is incompetent or untrustworthy in every other capacity. Localization thus becomes the stronghold of mediocrity, the sure avenue to office of the second-and third-rate man,--he who wishes always to enjoy his share of a little brief authority, to have, he also, a taste of public life. In this respect our American system is, I submit, manifestly and incomparably inferior to the system of parliamentary election existing in Great Britain, itself open to grave criticism. In Great Britain the public man seeks the constituency wherever he can find it; or the constituency seeks its representative wherever it recognizes him. The present Prime Minister of Great Britain, for instance, represents a small Scotch constituency in which he never resided, but by which he was elected more than twenty years ago, and through which he has since consecutively remained in public life. On the other hand, look at the waste and extravagance of the system now and traditionally in use with us. To get into public life a man must not only be in sympathy with the majority of the citizens of the locality in which he lives, but he must continue to be in sympathy with that majority; or, at any election, like Mr. Cannon in the election just held, where for any passing cause a majority of his neighbors in the locality in which he lives may fail to support him, he must go into retirement. I cannot here enlarge on this topic, vital as I see it; I have neither space nor time, and must, therefore, needs content myself with the "hints" of Paracelsus. I will merely say that as an outcome this localized majority system practically disfranchises the more intelligent and the more disinterested, the more individual and independent of every constituency. It reduces their influence, and negatives their action. It operates in like fashion everywhere. My field of observation has been at home, here in America; but it has been the same in France. For instance, while preparing this address I came across the following in that most respectable sheet, the London *Athenaum*. A very competent Frenchman was there criticising a recent book entitled "Idealism in France." Reference was by him made to what, in France, is known as the "*scrutin d'arrondissement,*" or, in other words, the district representative system. The critic declares that this system has there "created a party machine which has brought the country under the sway of a sort of

Radical-Socialist Tammany, and bound together the voter and the deputy by a tie of mutual corruption, the candidate promising Government favors to the elector in return for his vote, and the elector supporting the candidate who promises most. Hence a policy in which ideas and ideals are forgotten for personal and local interests, as each candidate strives to outbid his rivals in the bribes that he offers to his constituents. Hence, finally, a general lowering in the tone of French home politics, every question being made subservient by the deputies to that of their reëlection."

I would respectfully inquire if the above does not apply word for word to the condition of affairs with which we are familiar in America.

But let me here again cite a concrete case, still fresh in memory; nothing in abstract discussion tells so much. Take the late Carl Schurz. If there was one man in our public life since 1865 who showed a genius for the parliamentary career, and who in six short years in the United States Senate--a single term--displayed there constructive legislating qualities of the highest order, it was Carl Schurz. Yet at the end of that single senatorial term, for local and temporary reasons he failed to obtain the support of a majority, or the support of anything approaching a majority, of those composing the constituency upon which he depended. Consequently he was retired from that parliamentary position necessary for the accomplishment, through him, of best public results. Yet at that very time there was no man in the United States who commanded so large and so personal a constituency as Carl Schurz; for he represented the entire Germanic element in the United States. Distributed as that element was, however, with its vote localized under our law, unwritten as well as statutory, there was no possibility of any constituency so concentrating itself that Carl Schurz could be kept in the position where he could continue to render services of the greatest possible value to the country. I, therefore, confidently here submit a doubt whether human ingenuity could devise any system calculated to lead to a greater waste of parliamentary ability, or more effectually keep from the front and position of influence that legislative superiority which was the arm of Aristotle to secure. "Cant-patriotism," as your Francis Lieber termed it; and, on this score, he waxed eloquent. "Do we not live in a world of cant," he wrote from Columbia here to a friend at the North seventy-five years ago, "that cant-patriotism which plumes itself in selecting men from within the State confines only. The truer a nation is, the more essentially it is elevated, the more it disregards petty considerations, and takes the true and the good from whatever quarter it may come. Look at history and you find the proof. Look around you, where you are, and you find it now." And, were Lieber living to-day, he would find a striking exemplification of the consequences of a total and systematic disregard of this elementary proposition in studying the United States Senate from and through its reporters' gallery. The decline in the standards of that body, whether of aspect, intelligence, education or character, under the operation of the local primary has been not less pronounced than startling. The outcome and ripe result of "cant-patriotism," it affords to the curious observer an impressive object-lesson,--provincialism reduced to a political system; what a witty and incisive French writer has recently termed the "Cult of Incompetence." Speaking of conditions prevailing not here but in France, this observer says:--"Democracy in its modern form chooses its' delegates in its own image.... What ought the character of the legislator to be? The very opposite, it seems to me, of the democratic legislator, for he ought to be well-informed and entirely devoid of prejudice." Taken as a whole, and a few striking individual exceptions apart, are those composing the Senate of the United States conspicuous in these respects? They certainly do not so impress the casual observer. That, as a body, they increasingly fail to command confidence and attention is matter of common remark. Nor is the reason far to seek. It would be the same as respects literature, science and art, were their representatives chosen and results reached through a count of noses localized, with selection severely confined to home talent.

I am well aware of the criticism which will at once be passed on what I now advance. Local representation through choice by numerical majorities within given confines, geographically and mathematically fixed, is a system so rooted and intrenched in the convictions and traditions of the American community that even to question its wisdom evinces a lack of political common-sense. It in fact resembles nothing so much as the attempt to whistle down a strongly prevailing October wind from the West. The attempt so to do is not practical politics! In reply, however, I would suggest that such a criticism is wholly irrelevant. The publicist has nothing to do with practical politics. It is as if it were objected to a physician who prescribed sanitation against epidemics that the community in question was by custom and tradition wedded to filth and surface-drainage, and could not possibly be induced to abandon them in favor of any new-fangled theories of soap-and-water cleanliness. So why waste time in prescribing such? Better be common-sensed and practical, taking things as they are. In the case suggested, and confronted with such criticism, the medical adviser simply shrugs his shoulders, and is silent; the alternative he knows is inescapable. After a sufficiency of sound scourgings the objecting community will probably know better, and may listen to reason; in a way, conforming thereto. So, also, the body politic. If Ephraim is indeed thus joined to idols, the publicist simply shrugs his shoulders, and passes on; possibly, after Ephraim has been sufficiently scourged, he may in that indefinite future popularly known as "one of these days" be more clear sighted and wiser.

None the less, so far as our national parliamentary system is concerned, could I have my way in a revision of the Constitution, I would increase the senatorial term to ten years, and I would, were such a thing within the range of possibility, break down the system of the necessary senatorial selection by a State of an inhabitant of the State. If I could, I would introduce the British system. For example, though I never voted for Mr. Bryan and have not been in general sympathy with Mr. Roosevelt, yet few things would give me greater political satisfaction than to see Mr. Bryan, we will say, elected a Senator from Arizona or Oregon, Mr. Roosevelt elected from Illinois or Pennsylvania, President Taft from Utah or Vermont. They apparently best represent existing feelings and the ideals prevailing in those communities; why, then, should they not voice those feelings and ideals in our highest parliamentary chamber?

As respects our House of Representatives, it would in principle be the same. I do not care to go into the rationale of what is known as proportional representation, nor have I time so to do; but, were it in my power, I would prescribe to-morrow that hereafter the national House of Representatives should be constituted on the proportional basis,--the choice of representatives to be by States, but, as respects the nomination of candidates, irrespective of district lines. Like many others, I am very weary of provincial nobodies, "good men" locally known to be such!

As I have already said, in parliamentary government all depends in the end on the truly representative character of the legislative body. If that is as it should be, the rest surely follows. The objective of Aristotle is attained.

Exceeding the limits assigned to it, my discussion has, however, extended too far. I must close. One word before so doing. Why am I here? I am here,--a man considerably exceeding in age the allotted threescore and ten--to deliver a message, be the value of the same greater or less. I greatly fear it is less. I would, however, impart the lessons of an experience stretching over sixty years,--the results of such observation as my intelligence has enabled me to exercise. I do so, addressing myself to a local institution of the advanced education. Why? Because, looking over the country, diagnosing its conditions as well as my capacity enables me, observing the evolution of the past and forecasting, in as far as I may, the outcome, I am persuaded that the future of the country rests more largely in the hands of such institutions as this than in those of any other agency or activity. Do not say I flatter;

for, while I can hope for no advancement, I think I have not overstated the case; I certainly have not overstated my conviction. There has been no man who has influenced the course of modern thought more deeply and profoundly than Adam Smith, a Professor in a Scotch University of the second class. So here in Columbia seventy years ago, Francis Lieber prepared and published his "Manual of Political Ethics." Adam Smith and Francis Lieber were but prototypes--examples of what I have in mind. The days were when the Senate of the United States afforded a rostrum from which thinkers and teachers first formulated, and then advanced, great policies. Those days, and I say it regretfully, are past. Unless I am greatly mistaken, however, a new political force is now asserting itself. I have recently, at a meeting of historical and scientific associations in Boston, had my attention forcibly called to this aspect of the situation now shaping itself. I there met young men, many, and not the least noticeable of whom, came from this section. They inspired me with a renewed confidence in our political future. Essentially teachers,-- I might add, they were publicists as well as professors. Observers and students, they actively followed the course of developing thought in Europe as in this country. Exact in their processes, philosophical and scientific in their methods, unselfish in their devotion, they were broad of view. It is for them to realize in a future not remote the University ideal pictured, and correctly pictured, from this stage by one who here preceded me a short six months ago. They, constituting the University, are the "hope of the State in the direction of its practical affairs; in teaching the lawyer the better standards of his profession, his duty to place character above money making; in teaching the legislator the philosophy of legislation, and that the constructive forces of legislation carefully considered should precede every effort to change an existing status; in teaching those in official life, executive and judicial, that demagogy, and theories of life uncontrolled by true principles, do not make for success, when final success is considered, but that, if they did lead to success, they should be avoided for their inherent imperfection.... The province of the University is to educate citizenship in the abstract."

It is the presence of this class, to those composing which I bow as distinctly of a period superior to mine, that you owe my presence to-day,--whatever that presence may be worth. I regard their existence and their coming forward in such institutions as this University of South Carolina, as the arc of the bow of promise spanning the political horizon of our future.

Through you, to them my message is addressed.

Milton Keynes UK
Ingram Content Group UK Ltd.
UKHW011146220424
441551UK00008B/849